Cindy Chen

KNOW THE WORLD OF
SHARKS
AND
WHALES
and other Strange Creatures of the Sea

by Rupert Matthews and Colin Clark
Illustrated by Jim Channell

KIBWORTH
BOOKS

First Published 1993
Reprinted 1994, 1997
Published by Kibworth Books
Imperial Road
Kibworth Beauchamp
Leics LE8 0HR, England

Copyright © 1993 Kibworth Books

All Rights Reserved

Printed in Belgium

ISBN 0-7239-0066-3

CONTENTS

THE GIANT SHARKS

All sharks' fins are quite rigid, and act as stabilisers, keeping them steady in the water. These, the largest sharks of all, are actually no danger to swimmers, nor even to other fish! They feed on tiny sea animals and plants, called plankton, which drift around in the world's oceans. All three species shown here are very rare. Scientists still do not know for certain how long they live, nor how large they grow.

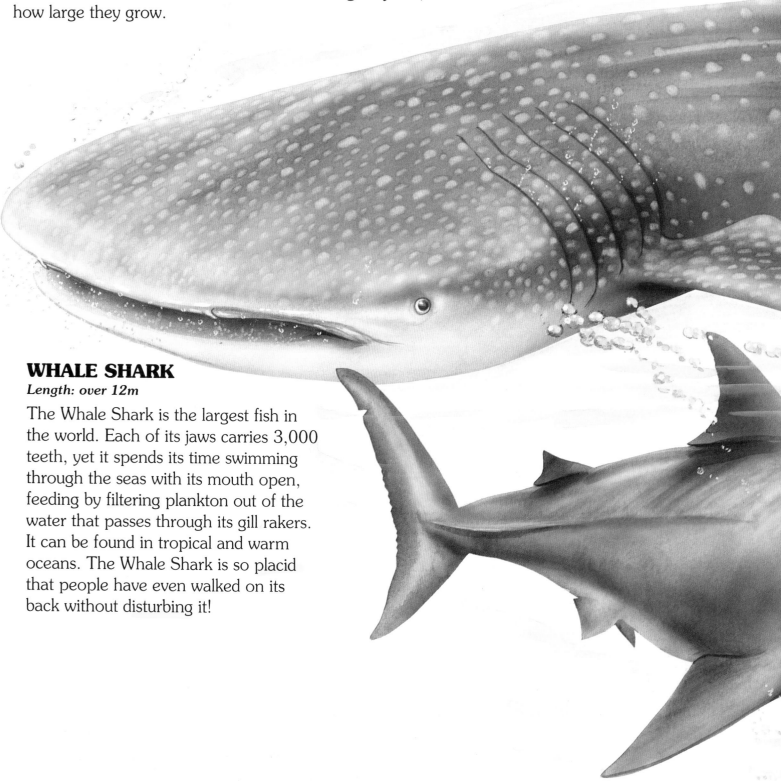

WHALE SHARK
Length: over 12m

The Whale Shark is the largest fish in the world. Each of its jaws carries 3,000 teeth, yet it spends its time swimming through the seas with its mouth open, feeding by filtering plankton out of the water that passes through its gill rakers. It can be found in tropical and warm oceans. The Whale Shark is so placid that people have even walked on its back without disturbing it!

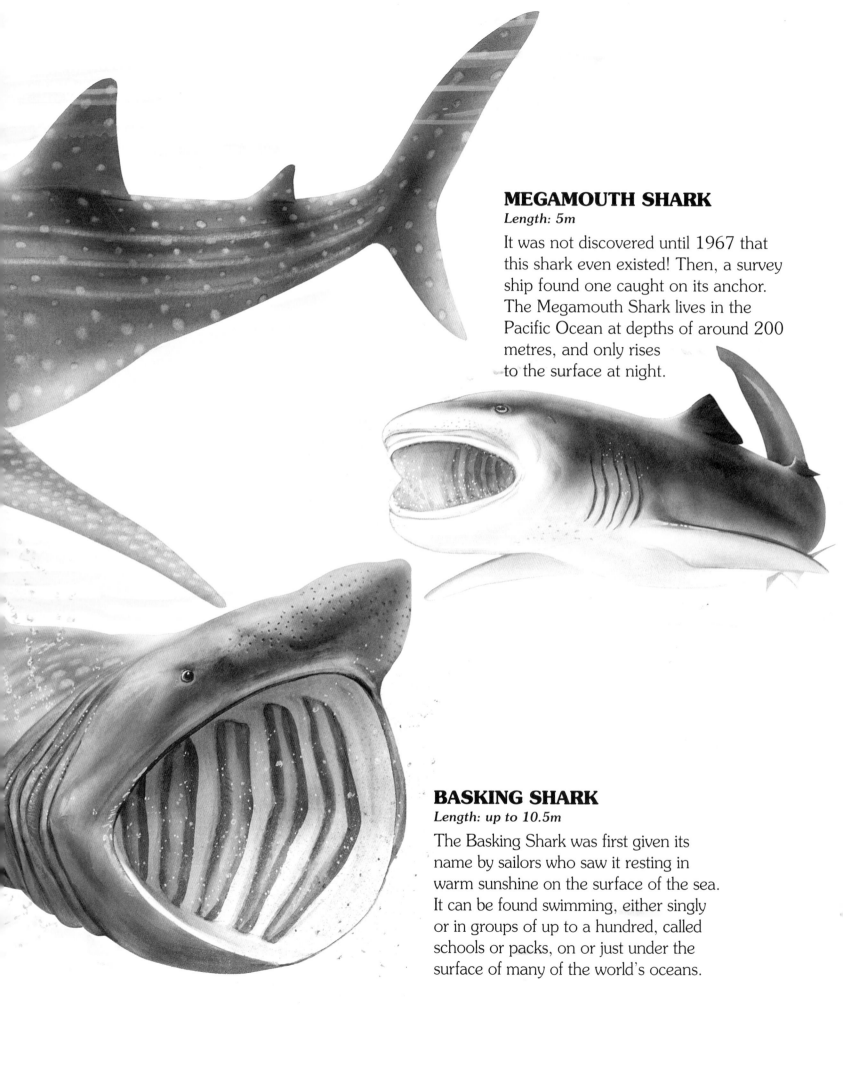

MEGAMOUTH SHARK
Length: 5m

It was not discovered until 1967 that this shark even existed! Then, a survey ship found one caught on its anchor. The Megamouth Shark lives in the Pacific Ocean at depths of around 200 metres, and only rises to the surface at night.

BASKING SHARK
Length: up to 10.5m

The Basking Shark was first given its name by sailors who saw it resting in warm sunshine on the surface of the sea. It can be found swimming, either singly or in groups of up to a hundred, called schools or packs, on or just under the surface of many of the world's oceans.

TERROR AT SEA

The larger sharks, because they feed on seals and other sea creatures, usually swim near the surface of the water where their prey is to be found. Their tails tend to be big in comparison to their powerful bodies. They travel thousands of kilometres in search of food, which they can detect by smell from far, far away. Only when they are close, do their eyes guide them in their onslaught. These sharks will attack human beings.

MACKEREL or PORBEAGLE SHARK

Length: about 3m

The name 'porbeagle' comes from the Cornish dialect and is of unknown origin. This ferocious predator can be found in open waters in the Atlantic and south Pacific Oceans, and in the Mediterranean and Barents Seas. A large, powerful fish, the Mackerel Shark, as its name would suggest, feeds in large numbers on mackerel, and on squid.

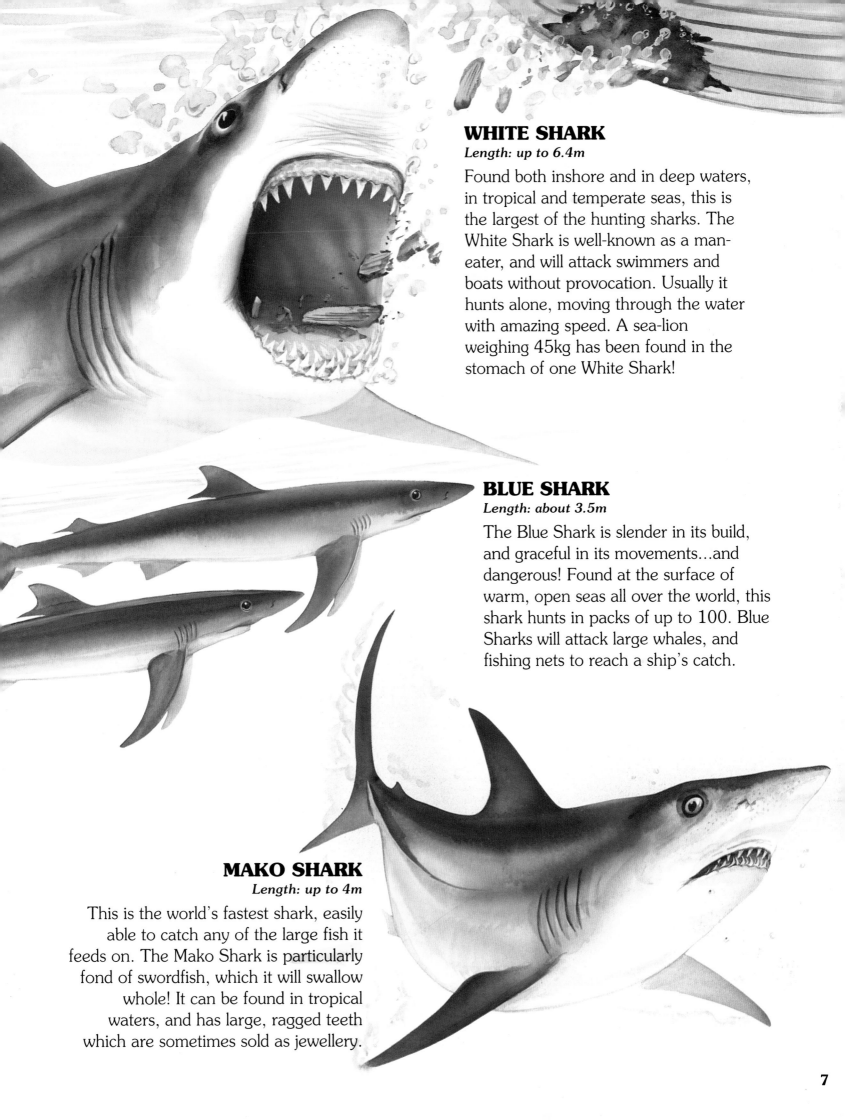

WHITE SHARK
Length: up to 6.4m

Found both inshore and in deep waters, in tropical and temperate seas, this is the largest of the hunting sharks. The White Shark is well-known as a man-eater, and will attack swimmers and boats without provocation. Usually it hunts alone, moving through the water with amazing speed. A sea-lion weighing 45kg has been found in the stomach of one White Shark!

BLUE SHARK
Length: about 3.5m

The Blue Shark is slender in its build, and graceful in its movements...and dangerous! Found at the surface of warm, open seas all over the world, this shark hunts in packs of up to 100. Blue Sharks will attack large whales, and fishing nets to reach a ship's catch.

MAKO SHARK
Length: up to 4m

This is the world's fastest shark, easily able to catch any of the large fish it feeds on. The Mako Shark is particularly fond of swordfish, which it will swallow whole! It can be found in tropical waters, and has large, ragged teeth which are sometimes sold as jewellery.

COASTAL KILLERS

Coastal sharks spend most of their time swimming slowly in waters close to shore. When attacking prey, they move quickly, but they give up easily if the chase is long. All three sharks shown here can be dangerous to man, as they will often come close to bathing beaches.

HAMMERHEAD SHARK

Length: up to 6m

This shark gets its name from the strange 'hammer' shape of its head. Its eyes and ears are on each end of the crossbar, sometimes a metre apart! They live in warm oceans, feeding off other sharks and fish, especially sting-rays. Large Hammerhead Sharks have been known to attack and eat men.

The Nurse Shark is the only Atlantic species of a group called the carpet sharks. It lives in shallow waters, where it will lie on the sandy sea bed, appearing to be asleep. But when a fish or crab comes into reach, the Nurse Shark will surge forward and devour the prey. Though normally peaceful, this shark will attack humans if it is provoked.

NURSE SHARK

Length: up to 4.25m

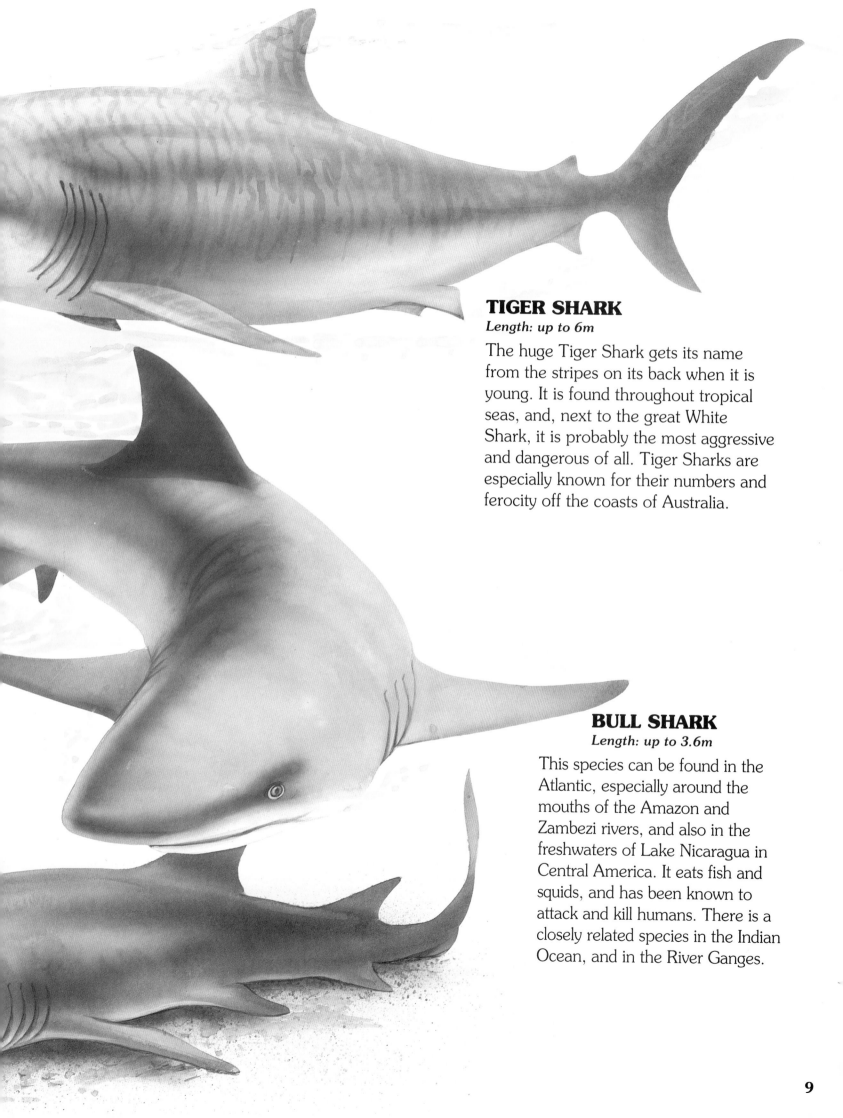

TIGER SHARK
Length: up to 6m

The huge Tiger Shark gets its name from the stripes on its back when it is young. It is found throughout tropical seas, and, next to the great White Shark, it is probably the most aggressive and dangerous of all. Tiger Sharks are especially known for their numbers and ferocity off the coasts of Australia.

BULL SHARK
Length: up to 3.6m

This species can be found in the Atlantic, especially around the mouths of the Amazon and Zambezi rivers, and also in the freshwaters of Lake Nicaragua in Central America. It eats fish and squids, and has been known to attack and kill humans. There is a closely related species in the Indian Ocean, and in the River Ganges.

THE LITTLE HUNTERS

Sharks are a varied group of animals. Some are large and powerful hunters, but most are small and they feed off prey that is even smaller. Whatever their size, though, they are true sharks, hunting with the killer instinct. Some lay eggs, while others may give birth to live young.

MONKFISH

Length: about 1.8m

The Monkfish is the largest of a group of sharks called the angel sharks. They are halfway between sharks and rays, with bodies that are flattened when viewed from above. The Monkfish has sharply pointed teeth, and lives around Britain on the sea bed, eating shellfish, rays, and flatfish. They give birth to between 9 and 16 live young.

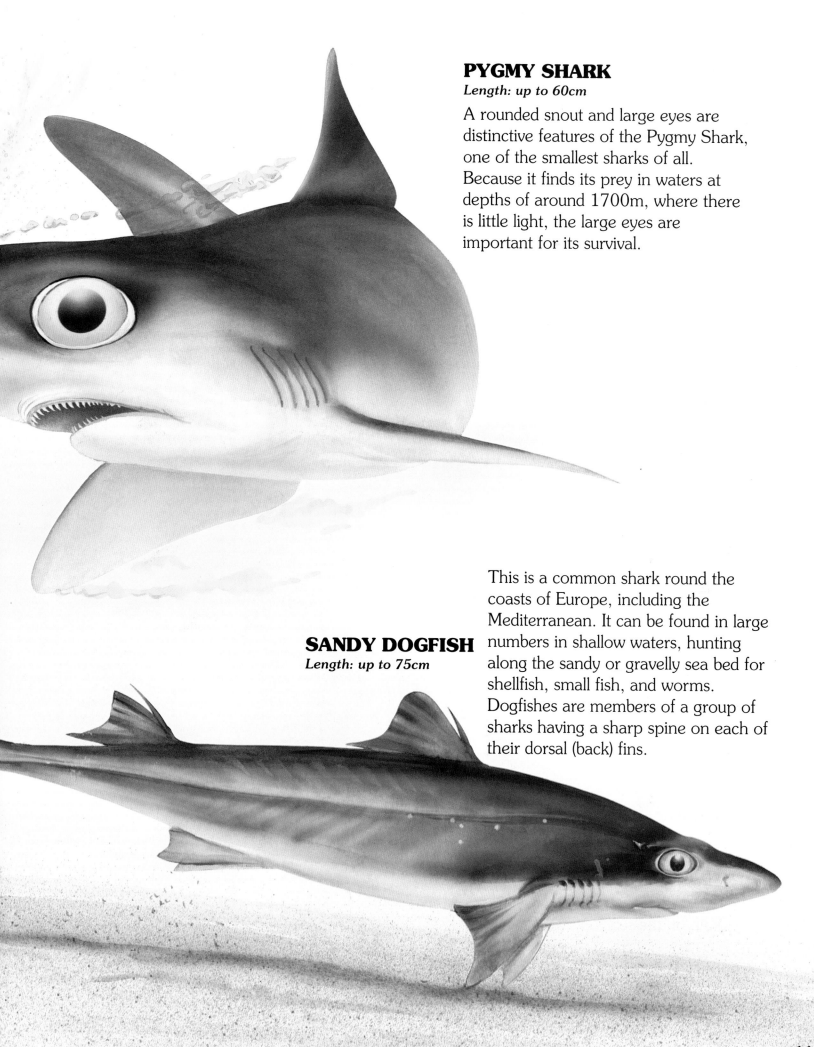

PYGMY SHARK
Length: up to 60cm

A rounded snout and large eyes are distinctive features of the Pygmy Shark, one of the smallest sharks of all. Because it finds its prey in waters at depths of around 1700m, where there is little light, the large eyes are important for its survival.

SANDY DOGFISH
Length: up to 75cm

This is a common shark round the coasts of Europe, including the Mediterranean. It can be found in large numbers in shallow waters, hunting along the sandy or gravelly sea bed for shellfish, small fish, and worms. Dogfishes are members of a group of sharks having a sharp spine on each of their dorsal (back) fins.

UNUSUAL SHARKS

Sharks have been swimming in the world's oceans for nearly 400 million years. Over that vast period of time, their shapes and features have changed considerably. The sharks shown here have evolved in unusual ways to fit in with their surroundings.

GOBLIN SHARK
Length: 3m

Fossils very similar to the Goblin Shark have been found dating back to 100 million years ago. Common in the western Pacific, these sharks are remarkable survivals of an almost extinct form. The snout has a peculiar development into a long, flat blade.

WOBBEGONG
Length: 3m

'Wobbegong' is an Australian Aboriginal word meaning 'shaggy beard', and refers to the growths around the mouth of this shark of the western Pacific. These growths, or barbs, help the Wobbegong to locate its prey. A carpet shark, like the Nurse Shark on page 8, the Wobbegong will squirm across damp sand to reach deeper water.

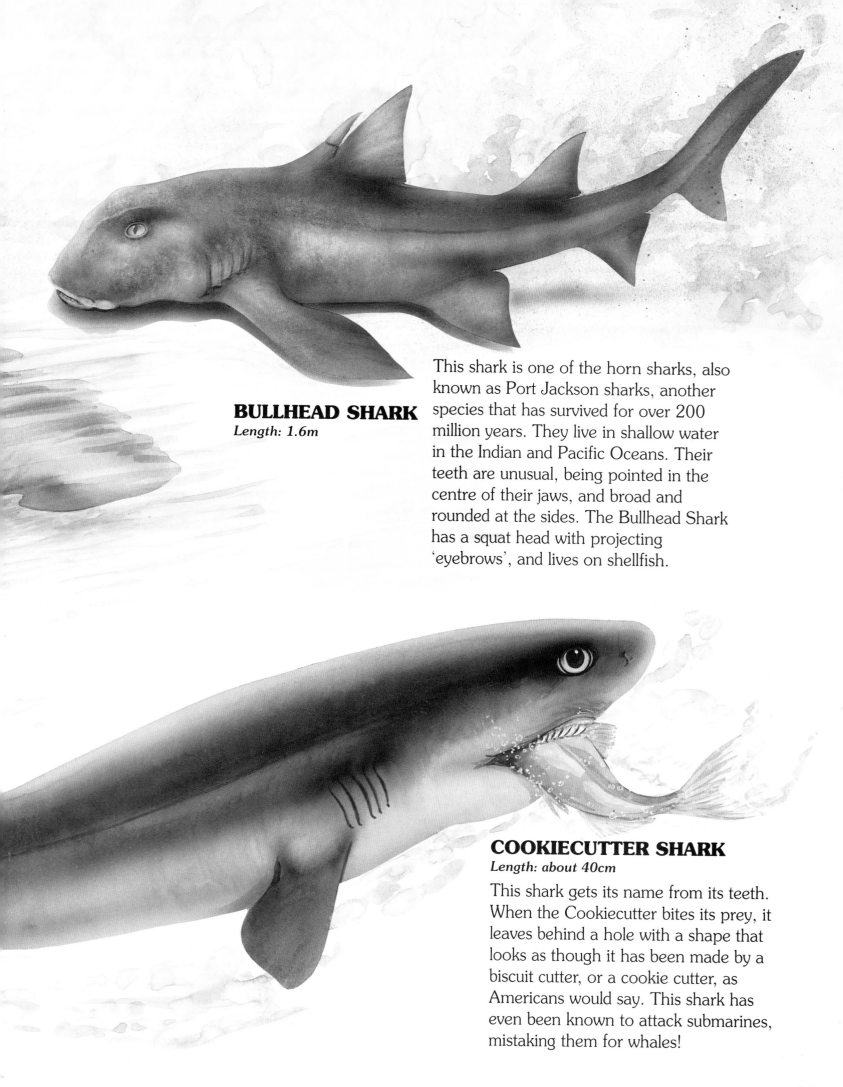

BULLHEAD SHARK
Length: 1.6m

This shark is one of the horn sharks, also known as Port Jackson sharks, another species that has survived for over 200 million years. They live in shallow water in the Indian and Pacific Oceans. Their teeth are unusual, being pointed in the centre of their jaws, and broad and rounded at the sides. The Bullhead Shark has a squat head with projecting 'eyebrows', and lives on shellfish.

COOKIECUTTER SHARK
Length: about 40cm

This shark gets its name from its teeth. When the Cookiecutter bites its prey, it leaves behind a hole with a shape that looks as though it has been made by a biscuit cutter, or a cookie cutter, as Americans would say. This shark has even been known to attack submarines, mistaking them for whales!

MAMMALS OF THE OCEAN DEPTHS

Whales are mammals which have adapted to life in the sea. In the distant past, when they were land-dwelling creatures, they had legs. In the course of time, the front legs have evolved to become flippers, and the back legs have disappeared completely. Whales breathe air, give birth to live young, and produce milk for their babies, or calves. They have horizontal tails. The Sperm Whales are those that have a reservoir of clear, waxy liquid, called spermaceti, in the nose. This adds buoyancy to the head, and makes deep diving easier.

GREAT SPERM WHALE
Length: up to 20m

The head of the Great Sperm Whale makes up one third of its body length, and much more than one third of its mass. The skin of an adult is patterned with circular marks, made by the suckers on the tentacles of the Giant Squid, with which the whale battles at depths of up to 3,000m! It finds its prey by echo-location. Because of man's hunting, this great whale is now quite rare.

PYGMY SPERM WHALE
Length: up to 3.4m

The Pygmy Sperm Whale is found in the warmer seas, and is smaller than some dolphins. It has a swollen nose, and a tiny jaw beneath its head. Slow-moving and deliberate in its movements, the Pygmy Sperm Whale is capable of diving to great depths in pursuit of squid and fish.

DWARF SPERM WHALE
Length: up to 2.7m

The smallest of the sperm whales is very shy, and, with its large, curved, back (or dorsal) fin, it has the profile of a shark. The rare Dwarf Sperm Whale lives in warm seas, and, like its huge relative, is able to dive deep and spend long periods underwater in search of its prey.

THE BIG-HEADS

There are three types of rare right whales in the seas today. The three species used to be numerous, but man has hunted them almost to extinction. They are slow-moving, and their bodies are so rich in oil that they float even when dead, so they were the 'right' whales to hunt! Right whales have no teeth. To feed, they draw huge amounts of water into their mouth, then filter out the plankton on which they live, through a series of horny plates, or baleen, that grow down from their upper jaw.

GREAT RIGHT WHALE

Length: up to 18m

This slow-moving whale can be found in shallow, coastal waters off a few parts of Canada, South America, South Africa, and in the Pacific. On the head, in front of the blowhole, there are crusted outgrowths, up to 10cm high, which are infested with barnacles, whale lice, and parasitic worms! The pattern of these growths is different for each whale.

BOWHEAD WHALE

Length: up to 20m

The largest of this group of whales, the Bowhead Whale has an immense head, taking up 40% of its total length. When feeding, these whales swim along the surface of the sea, mouths open, gulping in great quantities of water, until they have gathered enough plankton on their plates of baleen to make it worthwhile swallowing! Bowheads are the only large whales regularly found in the Arctic Ocean.

PYGMY RIGHT WHALE

Length: up to 6.4m

This is the smallest baleen whale, and lives only around the Antarctic continent. It is seldom seen, and is thought to be very rare. Whales of this species swim in an unusual way, moving the body up and down in a wave-like motion.

THE GIANT WHALE

The largest whale of all, and, as far as we know, the largest creature ever to have lived on earth, is the Blue Whale, weighing up to 178,000kg. It is long and slender in build, with a powerful tail that can propel it through the water at up to 30kph. Blue Whales used to be found all over the world, but man has slaughtered them so ruthlessly that relatively few are left alive. Blue Whale calves are fed on milk by their mothers, about 600 litres a day! This milk is so rich, that a calf, which is born weighing around 7,250kg, will double its weight in one week!

BLUE WHALE

Length: up to 32m

When feeding, a Blue Whale will consume around 4 million shrimps each day! Most feeding takes place in the cold seas around the poles, while mating and breeding occur around the equator. Blue Whales can dive and remain under water for as long as half an hour. When they surface, they blow used air out of their blowhole to a height of up to 12m.

THE FAST WHALES

The fastest whales are all members of a group called rorquals, a word that comes from the old Norse for 'red whale'. In fact, rorquals are not red at all! The Blue Whale on the previous pages is a rorqual. With their long, slim, powerfully muscled bodies, they are capable of speeds of 30kph. In springtime, they move from warm to polar waters, where they can feed on the plentiful harvest of tiny shellfish, which they gulp down by the tonne. After being hunted almost to extinction, most rorquals are now protected.

HUMPBACK WHALE
Length: up to 17.5m

This whale is very different from the other rorquals. The Humpback Whale has numerous lumps around its jaws, each with a hair growing out of it. It also has two enormous flippers, about 5m long. During courtship, a pair of whales will rise together out of the water, clasping each other with these flippers, then crash back down again. Humpbacks produce the longest and most varied songs in the animal world. After being nearly wiped out, the few remaining Humpbacks are now protected.

SEI WHALE
Length: up to 18.5m

The Sei Whale is distributed over all the world's oceans, except the very coldest. They eat about 900kg of food each day, plankton, fish, or squid, skimming them from the surface as they roll from side to side. Sei Whales are usually found in small family groups of four or five. Pairing is thought to take place for life. Sei Whales live for about 70 years.

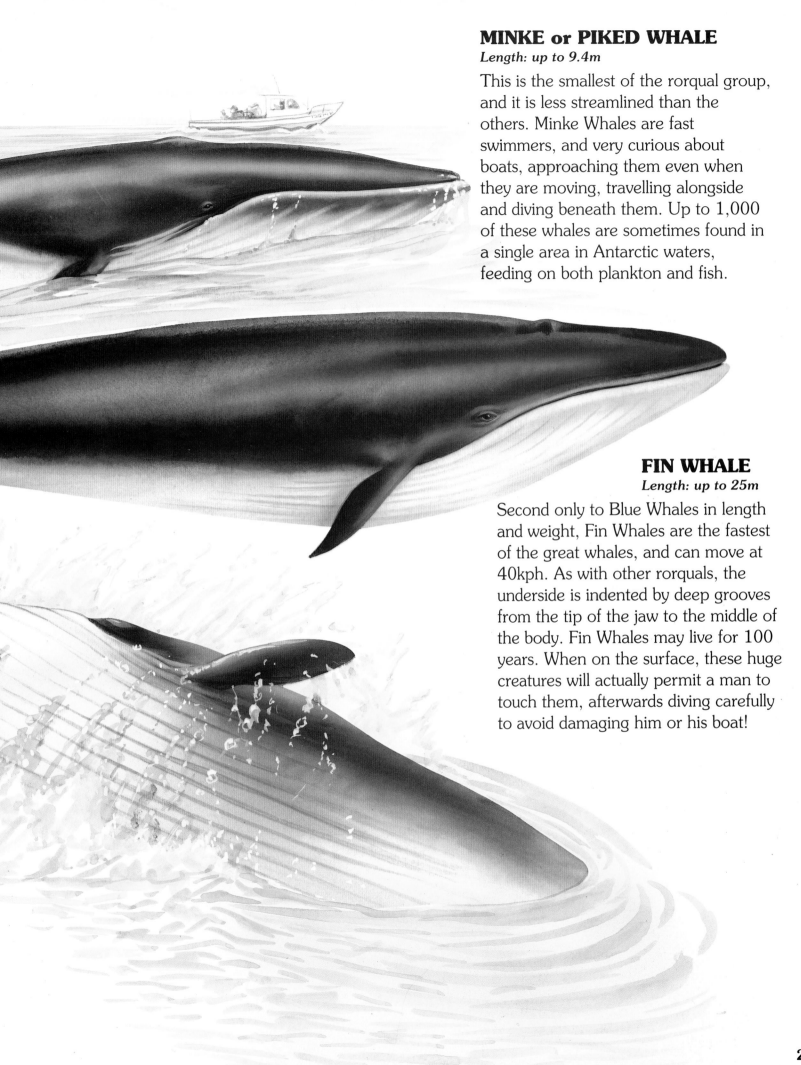

MINKE or PIKED WHALE
Length: up to 9.4m

This is the smallest of the rorqual group, and it is less streamlined than the others. Minke Whales are fast swimmers, and very curious about boats, approaching them even when they are moving, travelling alongside and diving beneath them. Up to 1,000 of these whales are sometimes found in a single area in Antarctic waters, feeding on both plankton and fish.

FIN WHALE
Length: up to 25m

Second only to Blue Whales in length and weight, Fin Whales are the fastest of the great whales, and can move at 40kph. As with other rorquals, the underside is indented by deep grooves from the tip of the jaw to the middle of the body. Fin Whales may live for 100 years. When on the surface, these huge creatures will actually permit a man to touch them, afterwards diving carefully to avoid damaging him or his boat!

'THE GREY SWIMMER ALONG ROCKY SHORES'

This was the name first given to the Grey Whale, by an American scientist, more than 200 years ago. This whale is in a species all on its own, somewhere between the right whales and the rorquals. We know more about the Grey Whale than we do about most, because there has been ample opportunity to study them on their mating and breeding grounds off the coasts of California. Grey Whales feed in the far northern seas, each year making the 20,000km trip south to California, the longest migration of any mammal, at speeds of 185km per day.

PACIFIC GREY WHALE
Length: up to 15.3m

Grey Whales feed on the Arctic sea bottom during the summer months. Little is eaten on the migration journey, nor at their destination. Calves are born exactly one year after mating, and the mothers and calves swim north again when the young ones are about two months old. Only when back in the Arctic will the mother break her 8-month fast! When a boat comes near, a Grey Whale will 'spy hop', or stick its head for about 2m out of the water to have a look at the intruder. They also 'breach', or throw themselves half out of the sea, many times in succession.

KILLER WHALES

There are three whales called 'killer', the Great Killer Whale, the False Killer Whale, and the Pygmy Killer Whale. Of these, only the Great Killer Whale really deserves the name, because it is a fierce predator. Even so, there is no record at all of any Killer Whale ever doing unprovoked harm to a human being. Remember this whenever you see a trainer in an oceanarium put their head into the mouth of a captive Killer Whale!

GREAT KILLER WHALE

Length: up to 9.75m

This streamlined whale has a heavy body, with large, paddle-shaped flippers, and a tall tail fin. It can swim at speeds of 50kph, and is to be found in all the world's open seas. They feed on a great variety of prey: squid, rays, sharks, seals, sea-lions, and other whales. One dead Killer Whale was found with 13 porpoises and 14 seals in its stomach! They live in family units of up to 50 members, working together to round up fish. Two Killer Whales have been seen tipping up an ice floe, so that a seal would slide off, into the mouth of another whale!

PLAYFUL DOLPHINS

There are many different types of dolphin in the oceans and rivers of the world. Here, and on the next two pages, we describe just a few of them. All small, toothed whales are sometimes referred to as dolphins, but the ones shown here are 'true', or beaked, dolphins. Dolphins have enchanted man from earliest times, with their intelligence, playfulness, and friendliness. They are famous for riding on the bow waves of ships.

COMMON DOLPHIN

Length: up to 2.6m

Common Dolphins are found everywhere, except in the coldest waters. In schools numbering hundreds, they can be seen leaping out of the water, catching flying fish in mid-air, and swimming at speeds of up to 64 kph. Dolphins will assist wounded companions and have even been known to help people in distress.

BLACKCHIN DOLPHIN

Length: up to 2.3m

Also known as Peale's Dolphin, after the first naturalist to identify it, the Blackchin Dolphin lives in small family groups around the southern coasts of South America. It is a friendly, little dolphin, feeding close inshore on fish, or on the seabed.

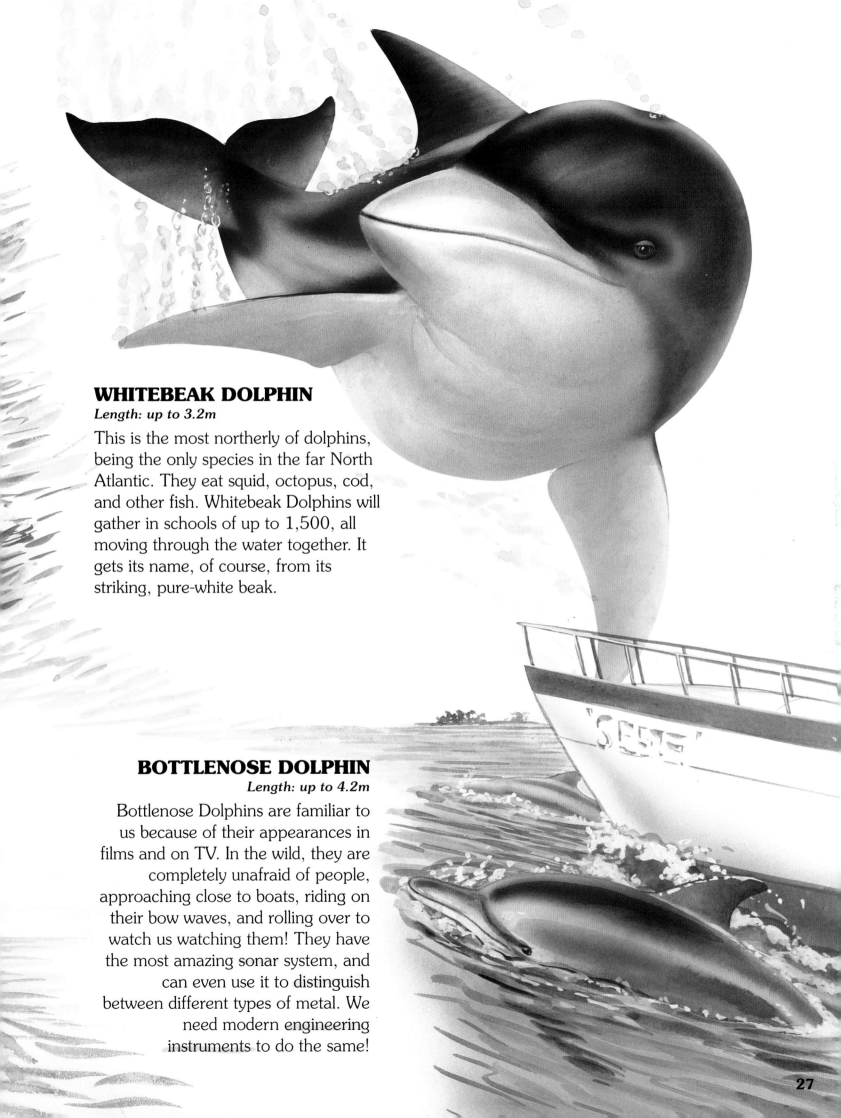

WHITEBEAK DOLPHIN

Length: up to 3.2m

This is the most northerly of dolphins, being the only species in the far North Atlantic. They eat squid, octopus, cod, and other fish. Whitebeak Dolphins will gather in schools of up to 1,500, all moving through the water together. It gets its name, of course, from its striking, pure-white beak.

BOTTLENOSE DOLPHIN

Length: up to 4.2m

Bottlenose Dolphins are familiar to us because of their appearances in films and on TV. In the wild, they are completely unafraid of people, approaching close to boats, riding on their bow waves, and rolling over to watch us watching them! They have the most amazing sonar system, and can even use it to distinguish between different types of metal. We need modern engineering instruments to do the same!

27

RIVER DOLPHINS

In some of the world's great rivers live dolphins that are very different from those in the sea. River dolphins are all small, with very long, narrow beaks. Because they live in muddy waters, their eyesight is generally poor, but they have remarkable echo-locating systems. By sending out loud clicks, and listening to the echoes, they can form a picture of their surroundings and locate their prey with complete accuracy.

GANGES RIVER DOLPHIN
Length: up to 2.45m

This dolphin lives in the great River Ganges, in India and Assam, from the mouth right up to the foothills of the Himalayas. Unlike other dolphins, this species swims on its side always, moving to an upright position only to breathe. Its slender beak can sometimes be 45cm long.

YANGTZE RIVER DOLPHIN
Length: up to 2.4m

In China, this dolphin is believed to be the reincarnation of a drowned princess! It lives in China's largest river, but, though it is protected, few are now left in the wild. Its beak turns up at the tip like a duck's. The Yangtze River Dolphin is a fish-eater, and very shy, staying well away from boats.

AMAZON RIVER DOLPHIN
Length: up to 2.7m

The colouring of this south American dolphin is an almost unbelievable, a shocking pink! Unlike its Asian relatives shown here, the Amazon River Dolphin has good eyesight, and will put its head out of the water to study a passing boat. It eats fish, including catfish and the fierce piranha. In the rainy season, these dolphins move into the flooded forests, but they always find their way back to the river when the water retreats in the drier weather.

HIGH-SPEED FISH

It is the speed of some fish that enables them to survive in the open seas. A few can power through the water at an amazing rate, far outstripping the fastest ship. High-speed fish have several features in common. Their bodies are streamlined, and muscular, and their tails are often large and pointed. These factors enable the fish to swim quickly, for long periods of time.

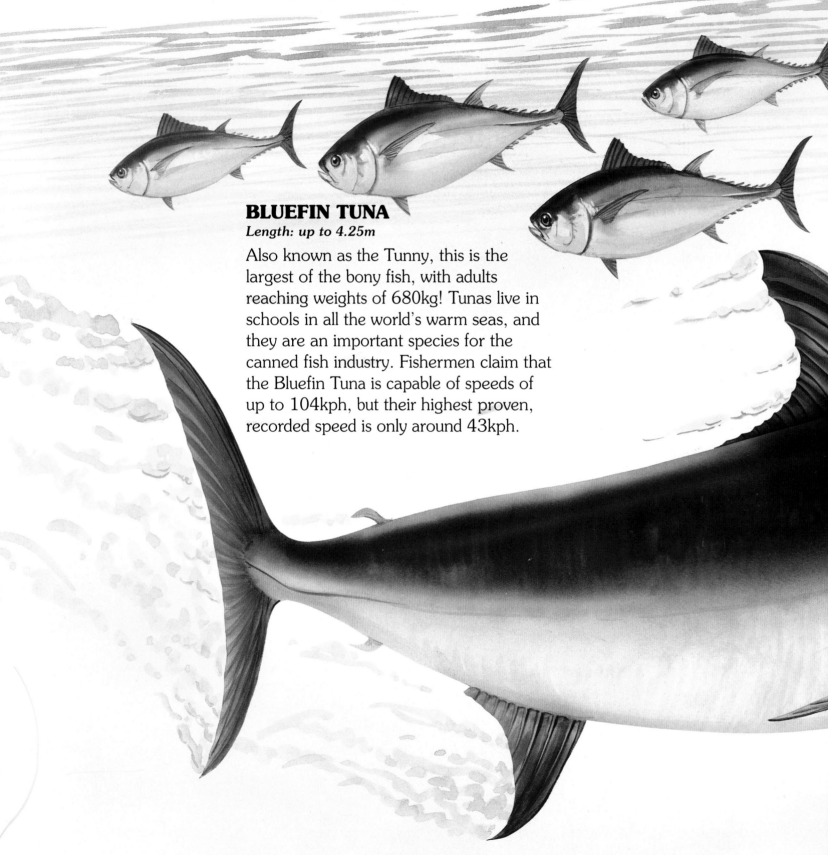

BLUEFIN TUNA
Length: up to 4.25m

Also known as the Tunny, this is the largest of the bony fish, with adults reaching weights of 680kg! Tunas live in schools in all the world's warm seas, and they are an important species for the canned fish industry. Fishermen claim that the Bluefin Tuna is capable of speeds of up to 104kph, but their highest proven, recorded speed is only around 43kph.

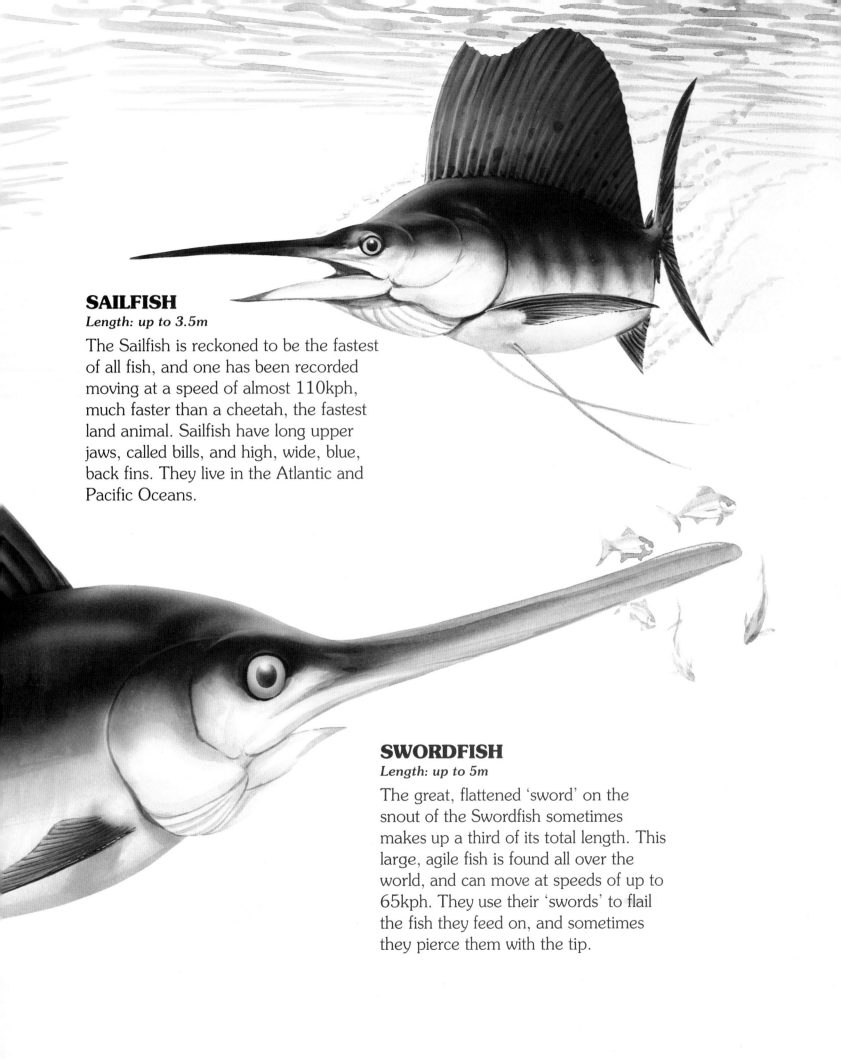

SAILFISH

Length: up to 3.5m

The Sailfish is reckoned to be the fastest of all fish, and one has been recorded moving at a speed of almost 110kph, much faster than a cheetah, the fastest land animal. Sailfish have long upper jaws, called bills, and high, wide, blue, back fins. They live in the Atlantic and Pacific Oceans.

SWORDFISH

Length: up to 5m

The great, flattened 'sword' on the snout of the Swordfish sometimes makes up a third of its total length. This large, agile fish is found all over the world, and can move at speeds of up to 65kph. They use their 'swords' to flail the fish they feed on, and sometimes they pierce them with the tip.

GRAPPLING GIANTS

Lurking in the ocean depths, there are a number of gigantic creatures which are rarely seen. In fact, science knows very little about these huge animals, except that they do exist. For centuries, they have featured in the stories told by sailors about their hazardous voyages.

GIANT SQUID
Length: up to 17.3m

The Giant Squid lives on the ocean floor. It is, like the octopus, a cephalopod, a word which means 'an animal with feet on its head'! Squids have 10 legs (or arms). Two of them are extendible, and can be shot out with great accuracy to seize prey, and draw it into the squid's sharp, beak-like mouth. Giant Squids grow to an enormous size, and fight battles to the death with Giant Sperm Whales.

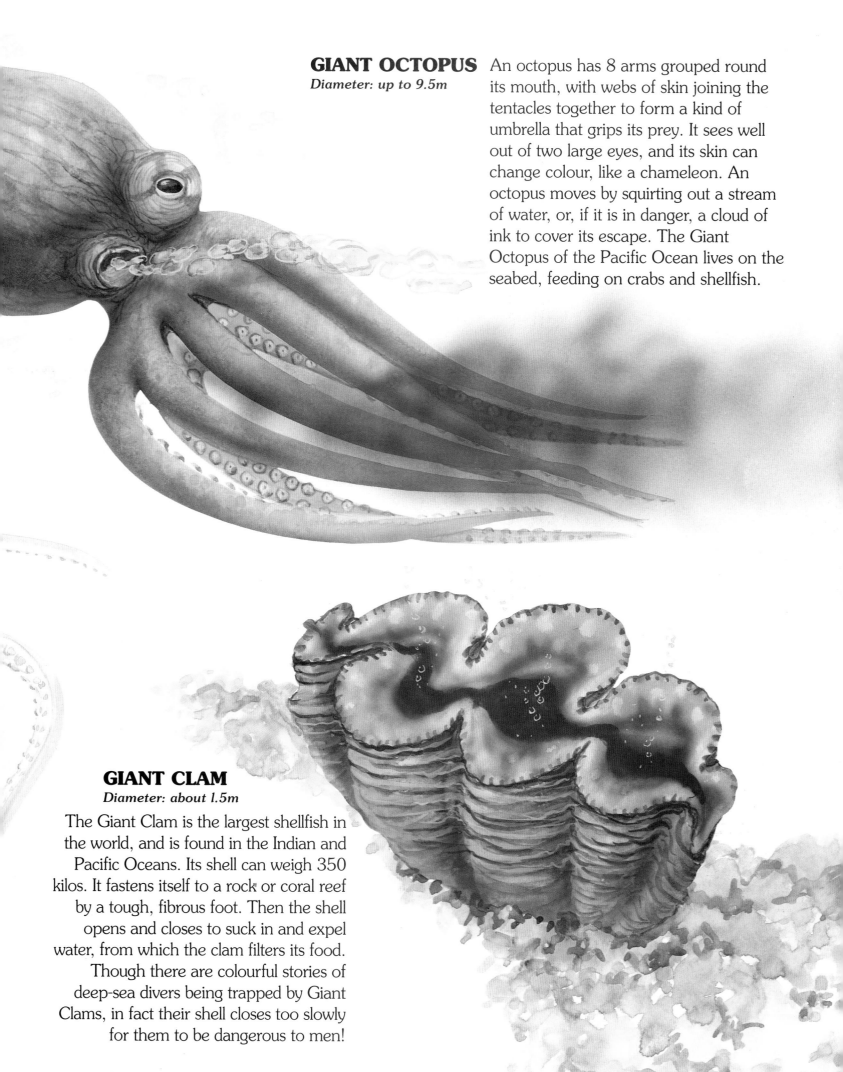

GIANT OCTOPUS
Diameter: up to 9.5m

An octopus has 8 arms grouped round its mouth, with webs of skin joining the tentacles together to form a kind of umbrella that grips its prey. It sees well out of two large eyes, and its skin can change colour, like a chameleon. An octopus moves by squirting out a stream of water, or, if it is in danger, a cloud of ink to cover its escape. The Giant Octopus of the Pacific Ocean lives on the seabed, feeding on crabs and shellfish.

GIANT CLAM
Diameter: about 1.5m

The Giant Clam is the largest shellfish in the world, and is found in the Indian and Pacific Oceans. Its shell can weigh 350 kilos. It fastens itself to a rock or coral reef by a tough, fibrous foot. Then the shell opens and closes to suck in and expel water, from which the clam filters its food.

Though there are colourful stories of deep-sea divers being trapped by Giant Clams, in fact their shell closes too slowly for them to be dangerous to men!

SNAPPING EELS

Eels are fish which have lost the fish-tail and most of their fins. Instead, their long bodies are very powerful, taking over the task of driving them through the water like snakes. All eels are hunters, attacking their prey on sight. They lay their eggs in deep waters, near the ocean bed, sometimes travelling thousands of kilometres in order to do this.

MORAY EEL

Length: up to 3.0m

Moray Eels are ferocious fish, with strong teeth, powerful jaws, and a savage bite. They live in cracks in rock or coral, or in wrecks, where they are safe from enemies. They wait for prey to come within reach, then dart out to seize it. Their fangs are poisonous in some species, and can cause a man's death. Skindivers must beware of them.

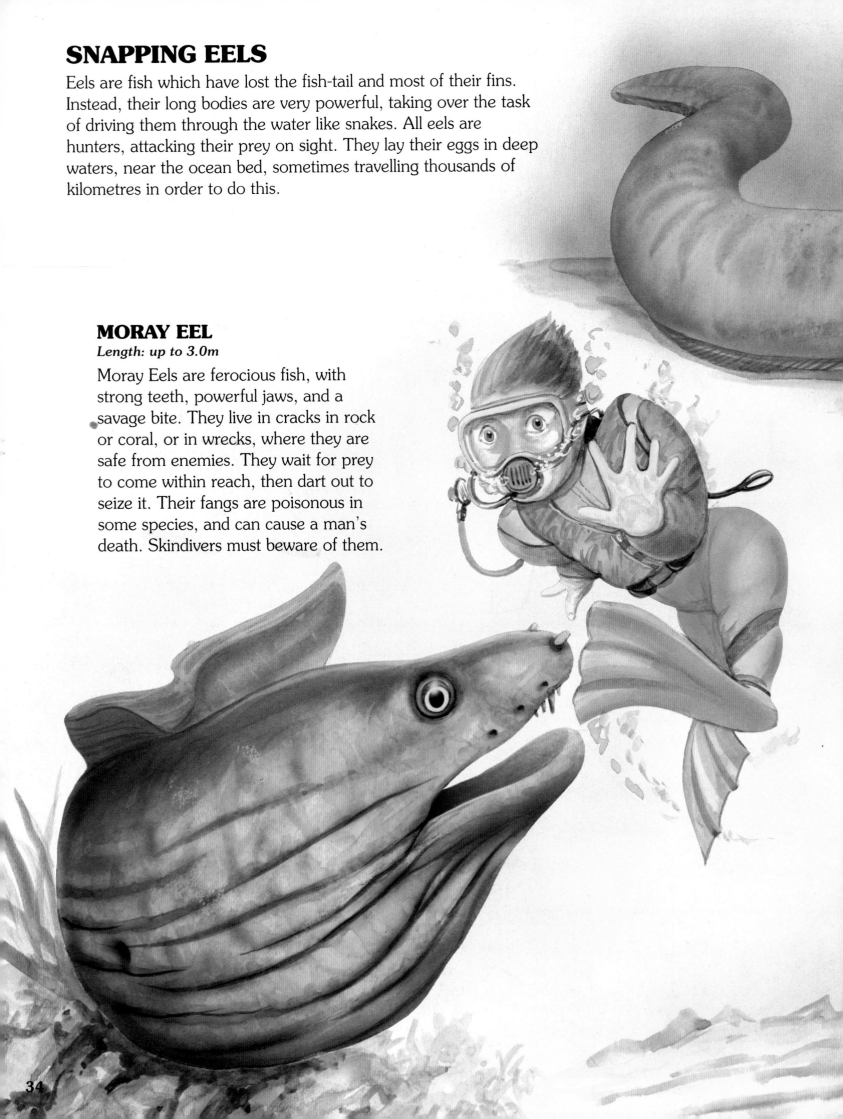

ELECTRIC EEL
Length: up to 2.4m

This is a freshwater eel of a different type to the others shown here. The Electric Eel is found in shallow streams on the Amazon and Orinoco Rivers in South America. Its body is lined with organs which generate a strong enough electrical charge to light a neon bulb. This charge will stun or kill any small animal within range, and even disable a man! The Electric Eel also finds both its way and its prey in muddy water by using its electrical charge as an echo-sounding device.

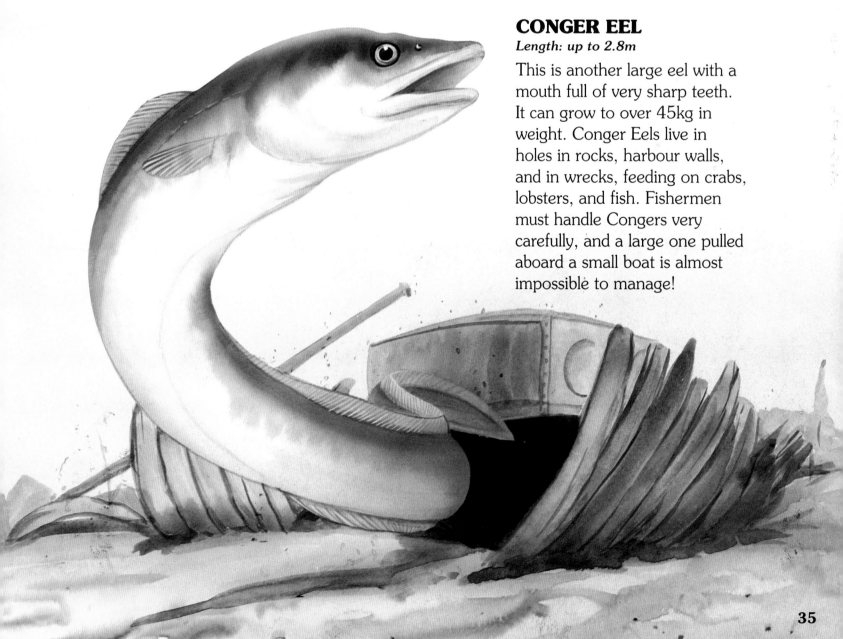

CONGER EEL
Length: up to 2.8m

This is another large eel with a mouth full of very sharp teeth. It can grow to over 45kg in weight. Conger Eels live in holes in rocks, harbour walls, and in wrecks, feeding on crabs, lobsters, and fish. Fishermen must handle Congers very carefully, and a large one pulled aboard a small boat is almost impossible to manage!

STRANGE NOSES

Some strange animals have developed in the seas as a consequence of evolution. Here we show some of the unusual noses which can be found, three fish and a mammal. Each nose serves a specific purpose for the species it belongs to.

SAWFISH

Length: up to 8m

The shark-like Sawfish is a relative of the rays. It is a bottom-living fish found mostly in warm waters. The long, flattened snout has sharp teeth on each side. The Sawfish uses its 'saw' either to stir up mud and uncover shellfish, or to lash about in shoals of fish, stunning and killing some of them.

DEEP-SEA ANGLER

Length: from 15 to 120cm

The many different kinds of deep-sea angler-fish live at depths of from 100 to 2,000 metres. Shown here is one which has a 'club' with a luminous tip to it growing from its nose, just like an illuminated fishing-rod. In the murky depths, this glowing tip lures other fish within range of the deep-sea angler's large mouth full of razor-sharp teeth.

NARWHAL

Length: up to 6.2m

The adult male Narwhal or Unicorn Whale has an amazing spiral tooth growing out of its upper lip, forming a tusk of over 2.5m in length. This tusk is always worn smooth at the tip, since the Narwhal uses it to dig for food on the seabed. This mammal is found in small groups in the most northern waters, but is now rare, because too many are being killed by hunters...not for food, but to turn their tusks into souvenirs!

SAW SHARK

Length: about 1.4m

The small Saw Shark lives mainly in southern oceans. Its long pointed snout is bordered on each side with large, sharp teeth. These sluggish fish use their 'saw' to root around in sand and weeds, detecting food by means of sensitive barbs beneath their chin.

SIRENS, MERMAIDS AND SEA-COWS

In old legends of the sea, sirens and mermaids are beautiful women whose enchanted singing lures sailors to steer their ships to destruction on the rocks. Maybe the legend was first born when an ancient mariner saw a sea-cow bobbing on the surface of the sea, cradling its young one to its chest. In scientific language, the two species of sea-cow belong to a group called 'sirenians'. Sirenians are the only water-dwelling mammals to feed entirely on vegetation. The name 'sea-cow' comes from their habit of browsing, like a cow, on underwater grasses. Sea-cows are descended, in the far-distant past, from the same group of land-dwelling mammals as elephants!

MANATEE
Length: about 4.5m

Manatees are found along the east-coast of America, from Texas to the Amazon, and on the coast of West Africa. They are big, heavy animals, weighing up to 700kg, living in bays, inlets, and large rivers. Their paddle-like tail fin is nearly circular in shape. Both parents care for the young, with one holding it while the other dives for food.

DUGONG

Length: about 3.6m

The few remaining Dugongs can be found in the Red Sea, the Indian Ocean, or round Australia. These slow-moving, almost defenceless, mammals live in small groups, grazing on sea plants. They have a wide, forked, tail fin, and the males develop two tusks, about 25cm long. Dugongs are now rare, as men hunt them mercilessly, for their flesh, hides, oil, and tusks!

39

SEALS WITH EARS

There are two groups of seals with ears: the sea-lions, sometimes called hair seals, and the fur seals, sometimes called sea bears. Sea-lions have a coarse coat of hair only, while fur seals have a thick undercoat of fur beneath the hair. All seals, and the walrus, evolved from land mammals in the distant past, their legs having become flippers. When swimming, eared seals use their front limbs as oars. On land, they can walk in a clumsy way with the aid of all four flippers.

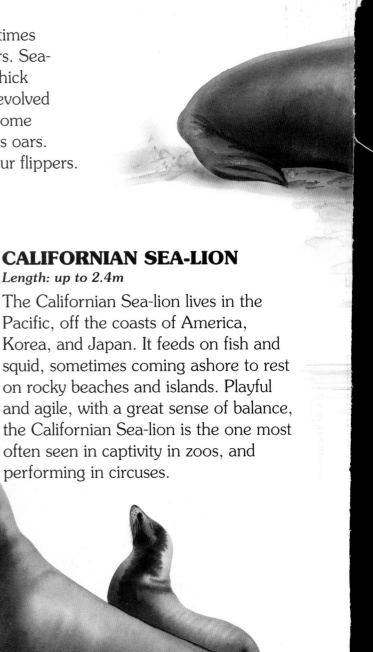

CALIFORNIAN SEA-LION

Length: up to 2.4m

The Californian Sea-lion lives in the Pacific, off the coasts of America, Korea, and Japan. It feeds on fish and squid, sometimes coming ashore to rest on rocky beaches and islands. Playful and agile, with a great sense of balance, the Californian Sea-lion is the one most often seen in captivity in zoos, and performing in circuses.

STELLER'S SEA-LION
Length: up to 3.5m

This is the largest sea-lion, weighing up to 1,100kg. It is found in the same areas as the Californian Sea-lion. In the mating season, thousands of Steller's Sea-lions gather in certain places, where the males fight each other to build up herds of females. Because of their weight, it is difficult for them to move about on land.

ALASKA or NORTHERN FUR SEAL
Length: up to 2.2m

This species migrates from the coasts of the Pacific Ocean to the waters of the Bering Sea for its mating season. There, on the icy Pribilof Islands, the males, the bull seals, fight to mark out territories, and gather the females into their harems. One bull seal may have a harem of up to 80 females. A female gives birth to one cub, a year after mating has taken place. This seal's fur is highly valued, by some people. Hunting is controlled to prevent the species from being wiped out.

SOUTHERN FUR SEAL
Length: up to 2.2m

The Southern Fur Seal is similar in size and appearance to the Northern Fur Seal, but its fur is not considered to be so valuable...except to the seal, of course! Nevertheless, it has been almost wiped out by hunters, and the remaining few are protected.

41

TRUE SEALS

Seals without ears are called true seals. Their rear limbs are swept back beside the tail, which propels them through the water with a side-to-side sweeping motion. They can only move on land by wriggling forward in a series of jerks. Although true seals have no external ears, they have fully functional inner ears, and acute hearing.

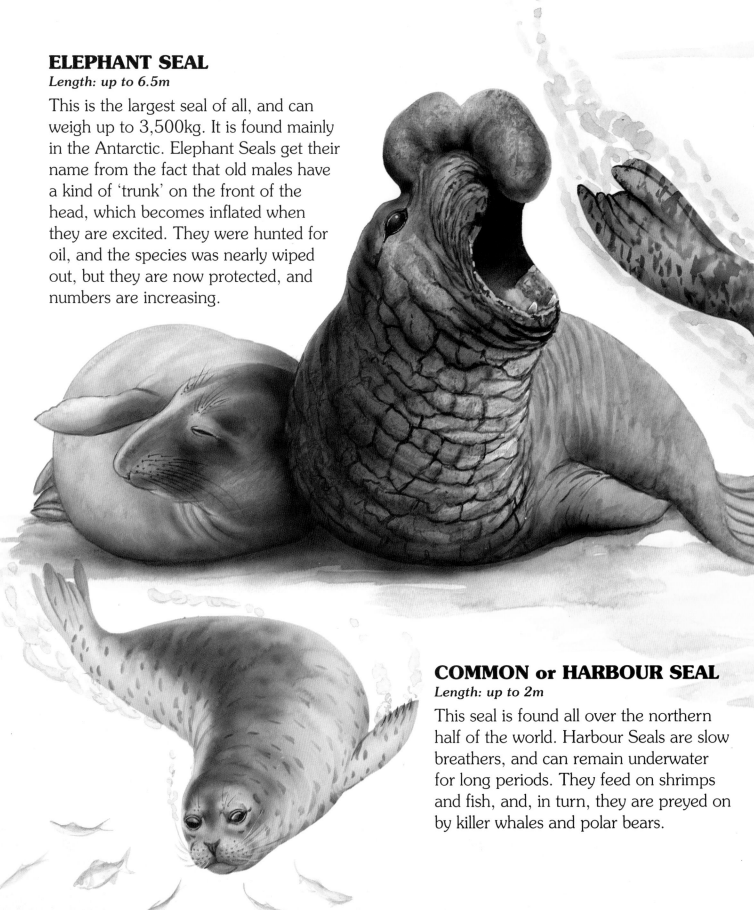

ELEPHANT SEAL

Length: up to 6.5m

This is the largest seal of all, and can weigh up to 3,500kg. It is found mainly in the Antarctic. Elephant Seals get their name from the fact that old males have a kind of 'trunk' on the front of the head, which becomes inflated when they are excited. They were hunted for oil, and the species was nearly wiped out, but they are now protected, and numbers are increasing.

COMMON or HARBOUR SEAL

Length: up to 2m

This seal is found all over the northern half of the world. Harbour Seals are slow breathers, and can remain underwater for long periods. They feed on shrimps and fish, and, in turn, they are preyed on by killer whales and polar bears.

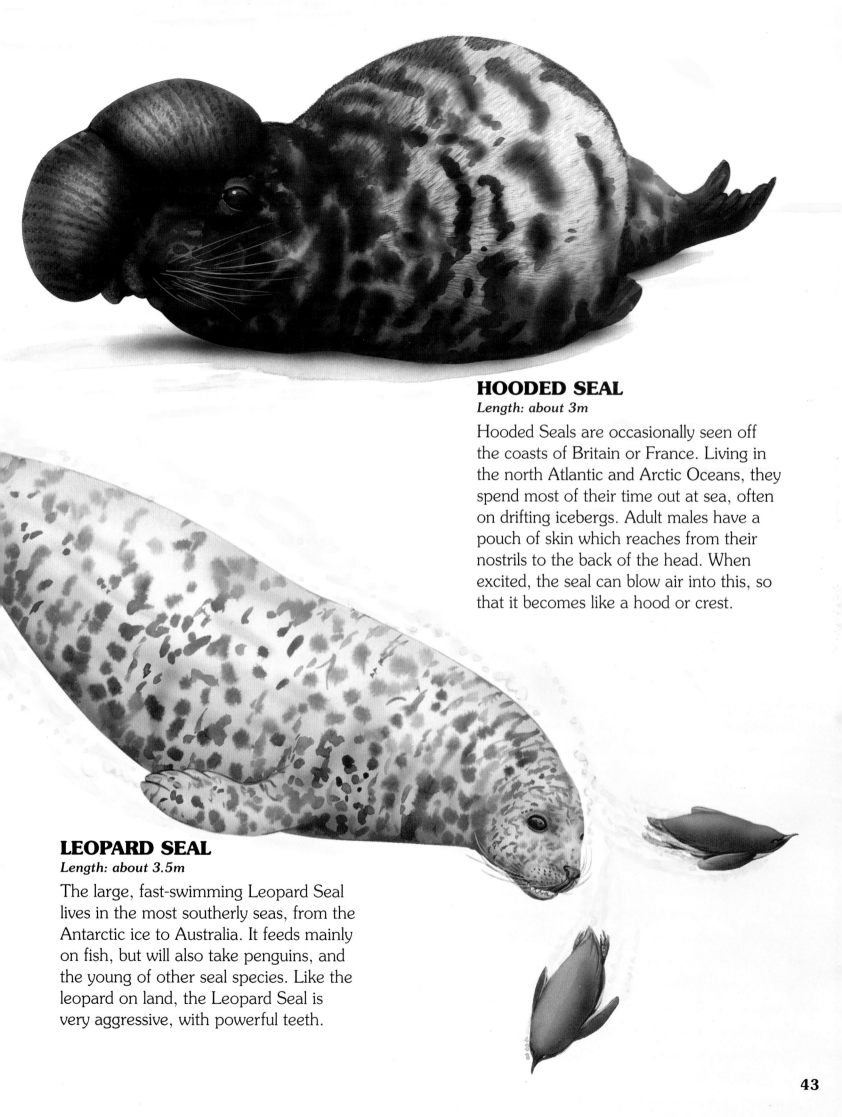

HOODED SEAL

Length: about 3m

Hooded Seals are occasionally seen off
the coasts of Britain or France. Living in
the north Atlantic and Arctic Oceans, they
spend most of their time out at sea, often
on drifting icebergs. Adult males have a
pouch of skin which reaches from their
nostrils to the back of the head. When
excited, the seal can blow air into this, so
that it becomes like a hood or crest.

LEOPARD SEAL

Length: about 3.5m

The large, fast-swimming Leopard Seal
lives in the most southerly seas, from the
Antarctic ice to Australia. It feeds mainly
on fish, but will also take penguins, and
the young of other seal species. Like the
leopard on land, the Leopard Seal is
very aggressive, with powerful teeth.

THE WALRUS

The Walrus is halfway between a true seal and a sea-lion. Like a seal, the Walrus has no external ears. Like a sea-lion, the Walrus can use its back limbs for moving about on land. It differs from both groups in its teeth. The Walrus has two enormous, downward-pointing tusks, which in males can grow to lengths of 80cm, and in females 50cm. These tusks are sometimes employed as weapons, but more often they are used for scraping shellfish from the sea bottom. The Walrus also has a tough, bristly moustache on its upper lip and cheek pads.

WALRUS

Length: up to 4.8m

As they are not such strong swimmers as
sea-lions, Walruses spend most of their
time in shallow water, or on ice floes or
beaches, where they gather in herds of
about 100. They live in Arctic waters, and
follow the ice line, moving south in winter
and north in summer. A Walrus makes use
of its tusks to haul itself onto an ice floe.
Sadly, as usual, the Walrus has been
hunted mercilessly, and its numbers are
greatly reduced. Some countries now have
laws to protect the remaining population.

MONSTER RAYS

Rays are closely related to sharks. Neither sharks nor rays are bony fish, having, instead of bone, skeletons which are made of gristle, called cartilage, which is rubbery and not as hard as bone. Neither sharks nor rays have the swim bladders that fish have. A swim bladder is filled with air and helps a fish to stay afloat even when not moving. Sharks and rays have to keep swimming all the time, or they will sink! Shown here are two different rays that grow to 'monster' size.

MANTA RAY
Width:up to 7m

The Manta Ray is the largest ray, and lives all over the world in warm waters. It is also called the 'devil ray' or 'devilfish', because of the 'horns' on each side of its head. In fact, these are just flaps of flesh which channel fish into its broad mouth. Mantas are harmless to men, and they 'fly' through the water with flapping movements of their huge fins, or 'wings'. A Manta Ray can weigh up to 1,300kg, yet at times they will leap right out of the sea, for no apparent reason!

EAGLE RAY
Width: up to 4m

The Eagle Ray gets its name both from
the eagle-like appearance of its head
with its heavily-browed eyes, and from
its 'flight' through water, which has been
compared to the flight of an eagle
through the sky. Eagle Rays live in
warm waters, feeding on the seabed on
clams and oysters. It roots up these with
its snout, and, as a consequence, it is
also known as the 'cownose' ray! The
Eagle Ray has a long, whip-like tail,
which, in some varieties, has a
poisonous spine at the end of it.

Index

Smith Books

$7.99

98 – 08 – 19

鯊魚和鯨魚書

Sharks & Whales(books)
and other strange creatures of
Robert Chen the
sea

陳建文武的

Aug. 19th, 1998, Wed.